BE A BLESSING

A *Spring of Refreshment* *on the Road of Daily Life*

Elizabeth M. Nagel

Ray Heuberger
232 E. Main
Sublimity, Or

Paulist Press
New York/Mahwah, N.J.

Cover design by Cynthia Dunne

Library of Congress Cataloging-in-Publication Data

Nagel, Elizabeth M.
    Be a blessing : a spring of refreshment on the road of daily life / Elizabeth M. Nagel.
        p. cm.– (IlluminationBook)
    Includes bibliographical references.
    ISBN 0-8091-4421-2 (alk. paper)
    1. Blessing and cursing. 2.. Christian life. I. Title.
    BV4509.5.N34 2006
    248.4–dc22

                                                                2006019571

Published by Paulist Press
997 Macarthur Boulevard
Mahwah, New Jersey 07430

www.paulistpress.com

Printed and bound in the
United States of America

Contents

TO

Sr. Barbara Bozak and her community, the Congregation of the Sisters of Saint Joseph of Chambery, whose hospitality and extremely generous financial support made it possible for me to complete a doctoral degree at the Pontifical Biblical Institute in Rome.

Acknowledgments

The inspiration to write about being a blessing comes from my parents, family, and all those who generously passed on God's blessings to me. Among these, I am grateful in a particular way to Bonaventure Zerr, OSB, and Jean-Louis Ska, SJ, who taught me the art of biblical interpretation, and to Dr. Robert Wicks and his wife, Michaele, whose mentoring and friendship remind me of the outrageously generous quality of divine gifts. I am also grateful to Saint Charles Borromeo Seminary at Overbrook in Wynnewood, Pennsylvania, for the one-semester sabbatical that allowed me the time to write.

I thank especially Monsignor James Mulligan of the Diocese of Allentown, Pennsylvania, whose constant encouragement, careful reading of the manuscript as it progressed, and thoughtful suggestions gave me the energy to continue working on it.

Finally, I am grateful to Shura Sullivan and Father Christopher Schreck who assisted me with editing and formatting the final manuscript.

CHAPTER ONE
The Unseen Divine Dimension of Every Life

The Biblical Command to "Be a Blessing"

God's first words to Abraham lay out the divine plan for his life.[1] In Genesis 12:1–3, God commands this common ancestor in faith of Jews, Christians, and Muslims to be a font of divine blessings for all the families of the earth. There is no missing the point, as five times in this short passage the Hebrew root bless occurs: "I will make of you a great nation and I will bless you...be a blessing...I will bless those who bless you...so that in you all the families of the earth will be blessed." Be a Blessing, the title of this work, may seem an odd phrase to those familiar with the *common translation of Genesis 12:2 from the Greek: "I will bless you...so that you will be a blessing." But the form in the Hebrew is, in most passages, actually translated as a command.[2] "Be a blessing!" delineates Abraham's required and active participation in God's plan to bless the human race.*

Lest we mistake a blessing for the occasional charitable act, let us glance for a moment at what constitutes *biblical* blessings. Many are tangible and do include such gifts as possessions, success, health, and feelings of well-being and harmony with creation. But the greatest blessing is the gift of human life. Why? Because more than other living creatures, we human beings have an unseen divine dimension.

Genesis 1 conveys this mysterious reality when it assigns God's making of human beings to the last day of creation and then only after some deliberation. The male and female are the highpoint of the whole show. Only they are created in the image and likeness of God (Gen 1:26–27). The rest of the cosmos provides the stage on which these partners, with their hidden divine dimension, are to manifest and represent the Creator. Genesis 1 claims that, no matter how effectively other living creatures, stars, galaxies, seas, or mountains inspire wonder about a power and majesty beyond their own, none of them can resemble God and manifest God's presence as effectively as can a human being.

Genesis 2 depicts human beings as the composite of the dust of the earth and the breath of life, which God blows into their nostrils (Gen 2:7). The ceaseless rhythm of the respiration that carries a person through life—the sigh of relief, the fast breath of excitement, the gasp for air that comes with physical exertion—attests to God's constant companionship. Perhaps we witness an unconscious realization of the great gift that is human life when, no matter how constrained and narrowed it becomes through illness, disaster, or oppression, one hesitates to draw that final breath and to give up.

Both Genesis texts insist that there is more to a human being than meets the eye. Every man, woman, and child transcends the physical body and shares in the existence of the invisible God, and the invisible God dwells within them. This union makes human life the greatest of all blessings and makes it possible for people to be a blessing for others.

This little book explores how God guides and works within people to help them be a blessing for others. It begins with an overview of the elements that are involved in being a blessing as these appear in Genesis 12:1–3; specifically, that one must go forth from a comfortable place, leave behind what is familiar, and follow God into unknown territory, all without knowing the final destination. Subsequent chapters explore how these elements play out in biblical texts that focus on forgiveness, on the extravagant quality of divine blessings, and on the fears and attitudes that prevent people from engaging and thriving on these realities.

Genesis 12:1–3 reads: "Now the Lord said to Abram, 'Go from your country and your kindred and your father's house to the land that I will show you. I will make of you a great nation, and I will bless you, and make your name great; so that you will be a blessing. I will bless those who bless you, and the one who curses you I will curse; and in you all the families of the earth shall be blessed.'"

"Go"

In Genesis 12:1-3, God's first word to Abraham is "Go." This unexpected command bursts into an otherwise ordinary life. Genesis 11:27-32 summarizes its few details: Abraham, his brother Nahor, and their nephew, Lot, set out with their father, Terah, for the land of Canaan, but settle along the way in Haran; Abraham marries Sarah who is barren.

We do not know exactly how Abraham receives the command to go. Does he hear words in his own language? Does he decide that God is directing him through incidents in his daily routine or by changes in the circumstances of his life? Or, does a piece of information, a chance remark, open his eyes to a new view of his situation, leaving him restless and dissatisfied with his current experience of life?

While it might be interesting to us to know how God communicates with Abraham, the biblical writer sees as far more important the simple fact that God initiates the changes that Abraham makes. Abraham, for his part, is convinced that God calls him out of his present situation and desires to set his feet on the path to an experience that his own limited musing could never imagine.

Leaving Behind the Familiar

Abraham's going requires specific separations, which in the biblical world entail formidable risks. He must, in ascending order of danger, leave his homeland, his clan, and his extended family. In other words, God calls Abraham to live the life of a refugee—when he is seventy-five years old!

First, Abraham must leave behind his homeland, the geographical setting, and the culture, which, like a job and a home, provide the comfortable setting for his daily routine. He must learn to function in a new situation, another culture, where even familiar gestures might have different meanings and where the local, ruling attitudes and priorities appear strange, incomprehensible, or simply wrong. The ways of God's presence and action in the new territory challenge Abraham's presuppositions and beliefs about his divine companion and divine ways.

Perhaps even more disorienting and upsetting than leaving his homeland and its familiar population is Abraham's severance from his extended family and from established relationships. To go is to leave behind the people whom he trusts and upon whom he depends in times of need, the friends who are always there to celebrate his joys and console him in his sorrows and disappointments, and with whom he in his turn rejoices and mourns.

In short, obedience to God's command to go requires that Abraham be willing to sacrifice what seem to be the sources of orientation, security, comfort, and meaning in his life.

Moving into the Unknown

In the biblical world, every journey is fraught with dangers. Even water, that most basic need in an arid climate, is a constant worry. No restaurants, rest stops, or convenience stores provide drinks at regular points along the road. Springs, rivers, and wells are sparse and are shared by local families or clans. If those in control are not inclined to hospitality, travelers can find themselves in danger of death. Even modern travelers to the Holy Land are often surprised to realize that keeping water at hand becomes their main preoccupation. They must either carry it with them or know where to buy it along the way. After one August tour, one participant realized that he had spent eighty dollars on water alone!

For protection from dangers of the road most biblical travelers—especially those of Abraham's age—depended on their immediate and extended families. It is this reality that generates the biblical preoccupation with begetting sons.

That protective role of male progeny was illustrated for me by an incident that occurred when I was living in Jerusalem during a time of some civil unrest. One evening, I stopped with a group of friends for ice cream at a little dairy store. As the shopkeeper prepared our cones, someone asked him if he worried about the way things were going. His reply was a very joyful and certain, "Why no! I have three sons! They will protect me." Where does that leave the seventy-five year old Abraham who has no sons when God commands him to go?

"To the Land That I Will Show You"

Abraham sets out without knowing his destination. He packs up his belongings—no credit card, debit card, or cell phone—and, filled with the faith for which he will become famous, goes as God commands.

Journeys with vague destinations are a common biblical metaphor for life with God—a convention inspired by the realization that God, and divine ways, are exceedingly different from human ones. While intellectual knowledge gives some understanding of divine ways, they are learned best from the actual experience of traveling with God to places that one is not naturally inclined to go.

An example of a typical biblical journey is that of the Israelites out of Egypt, through the wilderness, and into the promised land. Three experiences along the way illustrate how God teaches the people to trust in divine guidance and providence.

In Exodus 14, after the Israelites leave Egypt and arrive at the shore of the Red Sea, they look back to see Pharaoh and his whole army in pursuit. When their capture is imminent, they regret that they fled from Egypt to travel with God. But suddenly a path opens up before them in the most unexpected place: through the waters. And just as suddenly, after they walk through the sea, the passageway disappears. God custom-made it for the moment it was needed, and only for as long as it was needed.

Likewise, in the wilderness, when the people run out of food and water, they long to be back in Egypt where, in spite of their bondage, they did not have to worry about their daily bread. To provide for them, God makes water flow from the very rocks before which they stand and complain, "Is the Lord among us or not?" (Exod 17:1–7, Num 11:4–9). And for food, God instructs them to eat the manna, a natural phenomenon that they do not recognize as edible (Exod 16:1–35, Num 11:4–9). Like the provisional path through the sea, the manna provides nourishment only while it is needed during the wilderness segment of Israel's journey with God to the land of Canaan.

Just as God commands Abraham and Israel to "go," so in the gospels Jesus calls disciples to "come," follow him, and learn divine ways.[3] To obey his command is to run all the risks that Abraham's going sets in motion. It too results in a journey on which Jesus leads disciples beyond their familiar routines and into new circumstances.

These biblical journeys also involve alterations in the travelers' mental landscape, in the "givens" that provide their sense of order and control over life. As they move into new territory, they become aware that God is encouraging them to rearrange their priorities, to change ingrained attitudes, to jettison cherished perceptions and personal opinions, and to accept, at long last, realities that they have denied for their entire adult life.

Particularly in the gospel parables, as the disciples listen to Jesus teach, and watch him put his teachings into practice, they are amazed at how different his views and priorities are from their own. What he considers a pressing concern, they never think about. Behavior that makes him angry, they accept as an unfortunate given of life. Those for whom he shows compassion, they do not notice.

His list of concerns seldom contains any of their preoccupations. Eventually, they realize that, if they are to follow him, they must perform the most difficult of all human operations; namely, *change one's mind*.

These mental moves frighten, paralyze, and often anger even the spiritually brave, especially those whose current set of "certainties" constitutes their hard-earned barricade against life's complex and perpetual anxieties. Contributing further to the turbulence set in motion by these moves is their undisclosed destination, the unforeseen consequences that they set in motion. Only deep trust in their divine guide can give humans the courage to take a single step into a new place in their mind.

The potential tragedy, for both descendants of Abraham and disciples of Jesus, is that they trust God too little to risk making choices based on divine views of reality. Lacking faith, they flounder on fear and miss the thrill and privilege of experiencing the adventure of life as a journey with God.

CHAPTER TWO
The Context That Makes Forgiveness Possible

*T*he elements of being a blessing—going, leaving behind the familiar, and moving into new territory with God as our companion— shape situations that call for forgiveness. Genesis 32–33 shows how divine blessing makes it possible for two brothers, who also represent two nations, to come face to face after years of unresolved enmity. Matthew 18:23–35 displays Jesus' view that passing on his blessing of forgiveness to others is a matter of life and death, for those immediately concerned and for the entire community; this passage we will explore in the next chapter. Each of these biblical passages takes surprising turns, which lead to *insights that inspire readers to take on the daunting project of forgiveness. Like many revelations about divine ways, these texts also impart the haunting apprehension that we seldom worry about life's authentic dangers.*

The meeting of Esau and Jacob in Genesis 32–33 illustrates how blessing makes it possible for Jacob, whose offenses drastically change Esau's life, to face his brother after years of estrangement. Presenting the encounter from the perspective of Jacob, the offender, reverses the familiar approach to forgiveness from the point of view of the one who is harmed by another. This text also recounts Jacob's shocking experience of divine companionship and his discovery of God in the most unexpected place, in Esau.

To appreciate this, we must look at what shaped the relationship between these brothers: the events that led to Esau's hatred of Jacob and Jacob's terrible fear of meeting his brother.

How Did Brothers Become Enemies?

We first meet Esau and Jacob as they fight each other in Rebekah's womb (Gen 25:21–26). This is a "children in the womb" scene, a biblical convention that foreshadows the adult relationship between two characters. Actions performed by children in the womb, and descriptions of their physical characteristics at birth, prepare readers to grasp the meaning of later events.[1]

In Rebekah's womb the twins fight so violently that she wonders if she can survive the pregnancy. Upon consultation, God explains to her, "Two nations are in your womb, and two peoples born of you shall be divided; the one shall be stronger than the other, the elder shall serve the younger" (Gen 25:23). When at last they are born, the first to emerge is red and hairy, so they call him Esau. His brother follows, grabbing Esau's heel, so they call him Jacob, or "Heel-grabber."

Esau and Jacob: Brothers and Nations

The birth scene preserves more than the family memory of a pair of twins. It depicts the ethnic connection between the nations of Edom (Esau) and Israel (Jacob), and preserves memories of their political history.[2] The less familiar identification of Esau with Edom is first made in the birth scene by the Hebrew words *'edom* (red) and *se'ar* (hairy). The latter, usually translated as "Seir," is the name of a tribe or territory within the land of Edom.[3]

The political history of Edom and Israel, a story of conflict, underlies the exchanges between the brothers in the book of Genesis. The prophet Obadiah sheds some light on the bitterness that fuels the rocky relationship between these geographical neighbors. His words help us to grasp the significance of Jacob's meeting with Esau in Genesis 32–33. In an oracle addressed to the Edomites, Obadiah describes the events of the fall of the southern kingdom, Judah, to the Babylonians around 586 BC. In the midst of that tragedy, some Edomites fight with the Babylonians against Judah and afterward occupy part of Judah's former territory.[4]

The prophet says:

> For the slaughter and violence done to *your*
> *brother Jacob*, shame shall cover you....
> On the day that you stood aside,
>   on the day that strangers [the Babylonians]
>   carried off his wealth,
> and foreigners entered his gates
>   and cast lots for Jerusalem,
>   you too were like one of them....
> You should not have entered the gate of my people
>   on the day of their calamity....
> you should not have looted his goods
>   on the day of his calamity.
> You should not have stood at the crossings
>   to cut off his fugitives;
> you should not have handed over his survivors
>   on the day of distress. (Obad 1:10–14)

Some Edomites did these things. They not only took spoils from Judah, but also captured fleeing refugees and either murdered them or turned them over to the Babylonians.

Jacob Changes Esau's Life

Two other texts, Genesis 25:29–34 and Genesis 27, add more strokes to the portrait of brotherly and national enmity. The first anecdote captures a scene from the twins' adult life. One time when Jacob is cooking a stew, Esau comes in from the field, famished, and says, "Let me gulp down some of that red [Hebrew *'edom*] stuff. I'm starving." Lest readers miss this connection between Esau and Edom, the writer adds, "Therefore he [Esau] was called Edom."

When Jacob insists that in exchange for the stew Esau give him his birthright, Esau responds, "I am about to die; of what use is a birthright to me?" The scene closes with an unflattering picture of Edom's ancestor: "He ate and drank, and rose and went his way. Thus Esau despised his birthright."

According to Deuteronomy 26:15–17, the "birthright" is the right of the first-born son to inherit a double-share of his father's possessions. When Esau has to make a choice between his stomach and future blessings, God's gift loses. All of this is, of course, a caricature of Esau/Edom by the Israelite writer of the text. At the same time, while the portrait of Jacob as one who manipulates his brother's weakness to his own advantage would delight its original audience, it is no more edifying than that of Esau.

Genesis 27 describes the last encounter between the brothers before they meet in Genesis 32–33. This is the famous story of Jacob who, with his mother Rebekah's planning and help, deceives his old, blind father, Isaac, and steals the ancestral blessing from Esau. The covering of Jacob's smooth skin with animal hide to make it "hairy" (Hebrew *sa'ir*), like that of Esau, recalls that detail from the birth scene and precipitates its significance.

God's announcement that the older child in Rebekah's womb would serve the younger becomes a reality when Isaac speaks the words of the coveted blessing over Jacob. These words ask God to bless him with fertility, and with the service and homage of other peoples and nations. One verse in particular sets the stage for Genesis 32–33: "Be lord over your brothers, and may your mother's sons bow down to you" (Gen 27:28-29). The fertility, position, and power that Isaac wishes to bestow on his favorite son, Esau, go instead to the grabby younger brother.

Thus does Jacob damage Esau's future prospects and diminish his prestige in the eyes of others. When Esau discovers the treachery, he weeps bitterly. Is it any wonder that he bears a grudge against the conniving "Heel-grabber" and promises himself that, after his father dies, he will kill him (Gen 27:41)? This vow of vengeance is Esau's last comment on Jacob until they meet in Genesis 32–33.

Jacob Travels into New Territory with God

Chapters 28–31 of Genesis follow Jacob into exile where God blesses him with two wives, two concubines, eleven sons, and many possessions as he works for Laban, his mother's brother. In this uncle, who tricks him into marrying the elder Leah instead of the beautiful Rachel whom he loves, he almost finds his match in deceitfulness. But as time passes, he manages to out-trick Laban and anger his cousins and consequently decides that it is time to move on. In this case, God uses his circumstances to lead him back to his homeland (Gen 30:25–43 and 31:3).

In Genesis 32, as Jacob leaves behind his familiar and profitable, though imperfect, routine in Haran, he goes again into the unknown. In addition to the usual perils of traveling in foreign territory, he is bound to meet Esau who, he fears, will kill him and his family.

To prepare for the encounter with the brother who vowed to kill him, Jacob divides his possessions in half and sends them in groups before him as an offering to Esau. The long lists of cattle, asses, sheep, male and female servants, two-hundred she-goats and twenty he-goats, two-hundred ewes and twenty rams, thirty milk camels and their young, forty cows and ten bulls, twenty she-asses and ten he-asses, and lastly of Jacob's immediate family, take up a lot of space in the biblical narrative[5] and perhaps bore modern readers. But the original hearers would have been awed by the size of Jacob's gift. A contemporary example of his possessions would be a long parade of cars, boats, bicycles, career and business possessions, bank accounts, investments, and furniture, all of which make up the half of a wealthy person's possessions.

Why are the lists of animals and people given so much space in the Genesis text? They represent the enormous blessing that God bestows on Jacob. The text could simply state that "God blessed Jacob and he shared half of his blessing with Esau." Instead, the detailed description of blessing after blessing impresses readers with God's prodigal generosity. That Jacob himself perceives his possessions and family as divine blessings is expressed in his prayer, which recalls them as evidence of God's covenant loyalty to him (Gen 32:11). Finally, the long list of possessions also shows how much Jacob is willing to give up in order to repair some of the damage he did to his brother.

Divine Companionship Is Not for the Timid

After Jacob completes his preparations, but before he meets Esau, he has a shocking experience of God's companionship (Gen 32:23–33). He is alone in the dark by the Jabbok River when a "man" suddenly attacks him. The fight rages fiercely the whole night long. As dawn approaches, the man's divine provenance becomes apparent when he touches Jacob's hip and cripples him, gives him a new name, and blesses him. As day breaks, the attacker disappears and Jacob limps off to meet Esau.

This text challenges our idyllic fantasies about human experiences of God. Where are the expected peace and light? Where are the pleasant, warm, and secure feelings? This kind of engagement with God is not for the timid, but for the persevering and courageous, and even upon these it leaves its mark.

The placement of this divine-human struggle in the narrative suggests that, from God's point of view, Jacob is not as prepared to meet his brother as he thinks, and also that he is afraid of the wrong thing.[6] While Jacob fears death at Esau's hand, God is concerned about the greater danger, that Jacob will meet his brother *unchanged*, that he will still put himself first and use others for his own ends.

His grasping and deceitful habits served him well enough as he grew into adulthood, supported his large family, and managed a very successful business. But, in God's eyes, they would be liabilities in the encounter with Esau. For this to succeed according to God's plan, Jacob must change. The suddenness of the assault on him and its occurrence in the darkness are clear signs of his unawareness.

The fierceness of the struggle indicates perhaps how much in the dark he remains. His divine opponent does not overpower him as they fight on through the night, a sign that Jacob's blind obtuseness is a match for God's effort to change him. He fights back until God makes it no longer possible for him to do so by dislocating his hip. But even then, Jacob does not release him. He hangs on, begging for—what else?—a *blessing*!

The attacker accedes to his wishes, and also gives him a new name. In God's view, he is now "Israel," because, the text explains, "you have striven with God and with humans, and have prevailed" (Gen 32:28). In other words, because he lasted! God admires him for his honest tenacity and for refusing to let his attacker go before he gets a divine gift for his efforts.

The identity of Jacob's assailant comes as a shock to him. Only as dawn approaches, does he realize that he was fighting in the darkness with God. He is so amazed that he survives the encounter that he names the site by the Jabbok River Peniel, which in Hebrew means "The Face of God."

This text illustrates the Bible's healthy respect for the gap between the immeasurably powerful God and frail human beings—a difference so great that any contact between them leaves humans changed.[7] Jacob limps away from the Jabbok. What humans see as a wound is really a badge of honor to commemorate his life-changing interaction with God. In memory of it, Jacob's descendants do not eat the thigh meat of animals because it is attached to the hip joint (Gen 32:32–33). This abstinence also reminds them that true Israelites imitate their ancestor's stamina and audacity as they too struggle in the darkness with God.

The Encounter in Its Context of Blessings

As the changed Jacob limps off to meet Esau, he walks for the first time before his family. In addition to the half of his blessings that he sent ahead to his brother, Jacob now treats him with the respect that the words of the blessing accorded to himself.

The blessing given him stated that "his mother's son," that is, Esau, would bow down before Jacob, yet it is Jacob who seven times bows to the ground as he approaches Esau. In the biblical world, this is the greeting of a vassal to his lord,[8] the seven times representing perfection or completeness, as in the seven days of creation and the seven seals in the book of Revelation. Even in our world, we have seven days of the week and the Catholic Church has seven sacraments.

What's more, in Genesis 33, Jacob addresses Esau as his superior. He calls Esau "my Lord" and himself his brother's "servant." His words, like the seven bows, bestow on Esau the honor that the blessing had brought to him and open the way to forgiveness.

The brothers meet in the peace that only divine blessing makes possible. The great cloud of God's gifts, received and exchanged, envelops the brothers, closing their eyes to human failings even while opening them to the extravagance of God's generosity. The two Hebrew idioms for biblical forgiveness—"to cover one's face" and "to lift up one's face"—cast light on the role of blessings.[9]

In Genesis 32:21, as Jacob prepares the parade of possessions for Esau, he thinks, "I may appease him with the present that goes ahead of me, and afterwards I shall see his face; perhaps he will accept [forgive] me." A literal translation of this verse makes even clearer the link between Jacob's gifts and their role in effecting Esau's forgiveness: "If I first *cover his face* with the gift that is walking before me, afterwards, when I see his face, he will *lift up my face.*"

Jacob comes to Esau "to cover his face," that is, to block Esau's vision with gifts so that he no longer sees Jacob's offense and, in effect, forgives him. For Esau then "to lift up Jacob's face" is to forgive, to take away, the shame and embarrassment that weigh down the offender's head so that he can once again walk with head held high.

Jacob urges his brother, "Please accept my gift [the Hebrew reads literally, *blessing*] that is brought to you, because God has dealt graciously with me, and because I have everything I want" (Gen 33:11). And so God's blessing provides the context for forgiveness. It is God who provides whatever it takes to repair the damage we inflict on one another. In this case, God's limitless providence takes Jacob the Heel-grabber, the deceiver, and turns him into Israel, who barters blessings for peace with his brother. Jacob's largess, even though motivated by fear, shows that he has at least become a worthy administrator of the powerful ancestral blessing.

The Face of God in the Face of Esau

When at last the brothers meet, Esau runs to Jacob, embraces him, flings himself upon his neck, kisses him, and weeps, each action recalling and, in a sense, reversing the effects of Jacob's offense. In Genesis 27:26–27, Jacob's kiss of his father helped to persuade Isaac that he was Esau. And, in Genesis 27:38, when Esau found out that Jacob had stolen his blessing, he also wept, but from anger and hatred. Now, in Genesis 33, when they meet over twenty years later, Esau kisses Jacob and weeps from joy.[10]

In spite of the extravagant gifts that Jacob gives him, Esau's eagerness to forgive his brother is surprising. It is also divine, as Jacob's words in Genesis 33:10 reveal: "No, please; if I find favor with you, then accept my present from my hand; *for truly to see your face is like seeing the face of God*—since you have received me with such favor." Could Jacob ever have imagined that he would find God's face, the face he saw at the Jabbok River, in the face of Esau?

To see the face of a forgiver is to see the face of God. In other words, the forgiving Esau is the unexpected "place" where God becomes visible to Jacob. Esau is like the burning bush from which God announces the divine plan to free Israel from bondage (Exod 3–4), or like Mount Sinai, the mountain that quakes and blows fire while thunder roars and God reveals the law that instructs mere mortals about divine ways (Exod 19).

None of the extraordinary biblical signs associated with these divine epiphanies appear in Genesis 33. Instead, what marks God's presence, for those with eyes to see, is the forgiving face and embrace of one brother who was once so angry with another brother that he decided to kill him.

CHAPTER THREE
Blessing amid a Ruined Life

*I*n the gospels Jesus goes about the divine business
of forgiving. He associates so often with tax collectors and prostitutes, those shunned by the
religious leaders, that he is known in Luke as "the
friend of sinners" (Luke 7:34). And in Matthew
18:23–35, forgiveness dominates Jesus' teaching on
community life. His parable of the unforgiving servant warns of the dangers in accepting God's forgiveness and continuing to enjoy other divine
blessings as well, yet failing to forgive others.

The kingdom of heaven, Jesus says, is like the
events set in motion by a king who settles accounts with
his servants. The king portrays God's views and behavior.

The servants are the community of Jesus' disciples who are privileged to work in the kingdom of heaven and who enjoy a constant flow of perks like divine grace and blessings, including forgiveness. The inconceivable amount of the first servant's debt is the irreparable damage that he did to the king, to others, and to the kingdom of heaven. The pittance, which the second servant owes the first, is an easily mended injury. Notice that the kingdom of heaven, as represented here, is not so much a physical place as it is the series of interchanges that occur among the members of the Christian community and God.

One must keep in mind from the start that in this parable Jesus is *not* teaching that people can harm others with impunity. Nor is he saying that because victims forgive perpetrators, these latter need not pay for the consequences of their actions against society. But Jesus is here concerned with another level of reality where his disciples personally forgive others as he continually forgives them.

Jesus' parable does more than restate his familiar command to forgive those who injure us. It provokes thought about a whole complex of elements that constitute the project of pardoning: why God forgives in the first place; how Jesus leads us into new territory when we forgive; human preoccupation with offenses committed against us; why we do not forgive; Jesus' response to our unwillingness to pardon others; how failure to forgive is a natural disaster; and lastly, that failure to forgive is evil.

Why Does the King Forgive the Servant?

The king—with what may seem the figure of divine dispassion—responds to the first servant's immeasurable debt by meting out a penalty. The servant cannot possibly pay, so the king orders his family and possessions (all his blessings) to be taken away and his life made miserable. Then something changes the king's mind. Something is suddenly more important to him than making the servant pay back his debt.

The parable describes the royal reversal this way. The servant falls on his knees and pleads for patience. He promises to do the impossible. He will repay the entire debt! The king, "out of pity," forgives the servant and lets him go (Matt 18:27). The king shifts his attention from himself and his losses to the servant's distress, and so rescinds his judgment.

The word that translates the Greek "out of pity" (*splagchnistheis*) means "to be moved in the depths of one's being," or at the least, "moved with compassion." It is a "gut" feeling, that inner lurch that comes with the deepest feelings. The king's compassion propels him past the servant's despicable behavior, past his arrogant claim that he could repair all the damage he did, and right into the servant's experience of pain and panic. Once there, in spite of the servant's seeming lack of contrition or remorse, the king cannot bear to inflict more suffering on him and simply sets him free. The servant's anguish at his self-created hopeless mess means more to the king than does his own irreparable loss.

Going with Jesus into Unknown Territory

Whenever we manage to shift our attention from ourselves to those who offend us, and to feel the slightest empathy with them, we set out with Jesus into new territory. When we go further and show others unmerited compassion, we image God whose likeness we bear. As we speak words of forgiveness, the divine breath carries them to our brothers and sisters.

In these moments, we are among the noblest beings in the cosmos, an intersection between heaven and earth. Everything about us—our thoughts, feelings, and actions—is merged with our invisible God and manifests the bond between us. We walk on earth, but not there only, for we are at the same time in Christ. We move in two dimensions, which, *pace* Plato, are not really so far apart after all.

Ironically, as we go with Jesus into the territory of others' lives we discover a haunting familiarity. As we grasp their predicament, we know that we have been there too and are not ourselves innocent of their faults. What does it matter if we never did precisely the same harm they have done? Their fundamental abuse of our human dignity is all too familiar to us from our own cavalier treatment of those whom we are prone to see, consciously or unconsciously, as our inferiors.

Adjusting to Life in a New Place

Even after we forgive those who harm us, we must continue to live among the ruins that they have made of our lives. The inner terrain of our minds, as well as the landscape of our daily routine, seems like a ravaged, war-torn land. Life is shabbier. Unexploded bombs and mines lie hidden, ready to do more damage.

Those robbed of the companionship of loved ones face life alone. Those who suffer continuously the physical and mental damage inflicted by another are left with limited resources and possibilities. Those who lose the respect and appreciation of coworkers and clients through the undermining gossip of others work less effectively than they could. Yet those who forgive like Jesus agree to live with just such changes.

As we walk with Jesus through the destruction, some of our fundamental views of forgiveness and our expectations of others shift closer to reality. We expected remorse from those who harmed us. Now we accept that they may be pleased with what they have done. We thought that justice required equal suffering for equal damage. Now we rejoice that, given our own countless offenses against others, in God's view this is not the case. We thought that strict justice was a more powerful response than empathy, which threatens to mitigate the offender's responsibility. Now we realize that Jesus prizes compassion above quid-pro-quo reckoning. We thought that, at the least, offenders would be grateful for our mercy and that, at the most, they themselves would become more caring for others. Now we accept the reality that they may remain unmoved by our goodwill.

Dag Hammarskjold caught the sense of what it is to live in the aftermath of another's outrage. As secretary general of the United Nations, he had daily opportunities to reflect on the millennia-old cycles of revenge that shape individual, national, and global relationships. Hammarskjöld concluded that the only thing that can break continuous cycles of destruction is forgiveness.

In his book *Markings*, he wrote, "Forgiveness breaks the chain of causality, because the one who 'forgives' you—out of love—takes upon himself the consequences of what *you* have done. Forgiveness, therefore, always entails a sacrifice. The price you must pay for your own liberation through another's sacrifice is that you in turn must be willing to liberate in the same way, irrespective of the consequences to yourself."[1]

The course of history, as well as of current events, shows that these sacrifices are too great for most mortals. Who can summon the humility and energy to release others from their debts of injustice, which may never be repaid, and set themselves on the daunting path of rebuilding their own lives? None but those who believe that the unseen God shares their deepest pain and that they can rely on their invisible but eternal and all-powerful partner. Filled with the conviction that God works out plans for their future happiness, they begin to transform the rubble of their lives into glorious manifestations of the kingdom of heaven. As they sweep away the debris and perform one little task after another, God's presence radiates through them ever more dramatically. Brand new and totally surprising blessings stream outward from them and into the lives of others.

As we follow Jesus up new steep trails that strain our stamina, the old terrain below us forms new patterns. They may not be as tidy or as pleasant as the previous ones. Perhaps they are incomplete, but even in their early stage, they have a charm and lure of their own. Our new elevation reveals more clearly the path that we were following, the one blazed by our old views of reality and expectations of how others should behave, and we now see that it was a tedious meander to nowhere. A chill of relief courses through us as we realize how close we came to wasting our life, to confining it to only a dull reflection of God's magnificent plan. How grateful we are that we see this now and not at the end of our life!

A Couple Who Followed Jesus through the Ruins

An event in Italy a few years ago says more than abstract concepts ever could about how sin's damage can be transformed into a manifestation of the kingdom of heaven. An American couple and their young son were on the highway when a car overtook them, a shot was fired, and the boy was dead. Even in their grief at so utterly senseless an act, their care for others prompted them to donate his organs to give renewed life to other children in Italy.

From the ruins of this little family came the divine gifts of compassion, life, and health for many others. Word of the parents' astounding magnanimity filled the Italian papers and magazines. A year or two later, the families of those who received the son's organs invited the couple to Italy to celebrate the lives of these other children. Two parents' dreadful grief is transformed into a sign of the kingdom for other families. They, like Abraham, were a blessing to another family of the earth.

Human Preoccupation with Slights and Offenses

The servant forgiven by the king in Matthew 18 *refuses* to go and do likewise. The parable focuses on this character with his tit-for-tat justice, a thriving and all-too-often acceptable pattern of behavior even in Christian communities.

No sooner had the forgiven servant left the king's presence than he "found one of his fellow servants" who owed him a pittance. The Greek for *found* (*'euren*) can mean both "found" and "came upon." Does he go looking for a debtor? Or does he just happen to bump into one? In either case, he seems a person ready to get even, a person who learned little from what just happened to him. Perhaps he spends his energy dwelling on old injuries, mentally reenacting scenes of how others humiliated and harmed him, nursing old resentments and magnifying the almost-forgotten missteps of others. He may serve the king, but he certainly does not imitate him. In fact, when the servant comes upon his peer, he is so moved with compassion *for himself* that he grabs hold of the second servant, starts to choke him, and demands, "Pay what you owe" (Matt 18:28). The startled debtor's reaction practically mirrors his own to the king's original sentence, but it has the opposite effect. The servant shows no mercy; he is intent only on getting back what belongs to him.

Perhaps we never physically grab and choke another person, but we find it easy enough to take advantage of occasions to get even with others in countless ways. We load our words with intimations and speak half-truths. We insinuate the unspoken, change the tone of our voice, lift an eyebrow, or shrug a shoulder. When we do such things, in Jesus' view, we are grabbing and choking the victims of *our* "justice."

Why We Do Not Forgive

Why does the first servant refuse to release his peer from debt? Why does he decline to pass on the king's forgiveness? Matthew 18:30 gives the simple answer. It reads literally: "He was not wanting to"! He acts like a self-centered child who never grows out of pleasing himself. He chooses not to control his emotions, chooses not to do what Jesus longs to do within him. He does not want to go into the unknown territory of another's panic. His actions proclaim that he cares nothing for following Jesus and is unaware of the privilege of his call to work in the kingdom of heaven. He casts aside the adventure of a lifetime in favor of a short-lived rush of revenge.

Failure to Forgive is a Natural Disaster

In Jesus' view, the act of the unforgiving servant is a community disaster. That is clear from the reaction of the rest of the servants in the parable. They are "greatly distressed" and run to the king to report the event. At first glance, their response is disproportionate and startling. Really, how often is the failure of one community member to forgive another perceived as a disaster by the rest? Look at ourselves. How often does every other matter—finances, power struggles, and ideological and liturgical preferences—take second place to someone's failure to forgive? Is such a spiritual failure ever as deeply distressing as the attacks on the World Trade Center and Pentagon on September 11, 2001? On the contrary, the refusal to forgive is so common in Christian communities that it can be called a "natural" disaster, like hurricanes and tornadoes, fires and floods, though these occur with less frequency. But the refusal to forgive is none of these impersonal events. It is a purposely chosen rejection of Jesus' call to show compassion to those who harm us.

The significance of the community's reaction is there in the Greek word *sphodra*, which means "great" or "deep." In the seven texts in which *sphodra* occurs in Matthew, it always marks an occasion in which either Jesus' divinity is recognized or his unique shocking view on a matter is presented.

In three of the passages, *sphodra* intimates Jesus' divinity: at his incarnation the magi "rejoice *greatly*" when they recognize Jesus (Matt 2:10); he is transfigured before three disciples who "fear *greatly*" as they see his divine glory (Matt 17:6); and his death is accompanied by cosmic signs that evoke "*great* fear" in the guards (Matt 27:54).

Three times, *sphodra* draws attention to one of Jesus' shocking views: that he must go to Jerusalem and be killed evokes the disciples' "*great* grief" (Matt 17:23); that it is easier for a camel to pass through the eye of a needle than for the wealthy to enter the kingdom of God evokes the disciples' "*great* astonishment" (Matt 19:24–25); and that one of his chosen twelve will betray him evokes their "*great* distress" (Matt 26:22).

And then there is our present text (Matt 18:31), where the "*great* distress" of the servants underscores Jesus' shocking insistence that those whom he forgives pass on his forgiveness to others. Exercising forgiveness is a task to take up a Christian community's time and energy, a task that its members set aside at their own peril.

Jesus' Anger at Those Who Show No Mercy

The failure to pass on divine forgiveness is a tragedy that undoes the king's sense of pity toward the first servant. The once-compassionate king now condemns the unforgiving servant to endless torture. The servant's refusal to "show mercy" is worse by far than his original failures, irreparable as they had seemed.[2] The haunting severity of the punishment unsettles readers who, busy about many good things, suddenly realize that, according to Matthew 18, all these mean little or nothing to God unless they are also willing to forgive daily.

Above all, note this: the king is not angry because the servant failed to *feel* badly for his peer, or to match the depth of his empathy. Rather, the king's anger is directed at the servant's failure to *do* something, his failure *to show mercy*. The king, like Jesus, demands more action than emotion from his servants.

There remains one last warning on the danger of not forgiving. Jesus warns his listeners that unless they forgive from the heart (Matt 18:35), they too will incur the divine wrath. Forgiving "from the heart," like showing mercy, is more a rational act than an emotional episode. The heart in the biblical idiom is the mind, the place where one reflects, weighs choices, and makes decisions. To forgive "from the heart" is to *decide* to do so and to stick with that decision. Sentimental pleasure or repulsion at the undertaking, liking or hating the very idea of it—these are irrelevant considerations. It is the doing that matters.

Not to Forgive—Not to Go—Is "Evil"

The unforgiving servant refuses to "go" with Jesus into the unknown territory of his peer's situation. He decides to forego the call to divine adventure and stay stuck in the rut of his human quid-pro-quo thinking. For his constant companions he chooses, not Jesus, but his favorite feelings of self-pity, self-righteousness, power, and vengefulness.

The servant refuses to enter the new territory of another's desperation, and so Jesus calls him "evil." Evil of this sort is what defiles a person from the inside: "For out of the heart [mind] come evil intentions, murder, adultery, fornication, theft, false witness, slander" (Matt 15:19). Few of us consider ourselves evil, simply because we do not think of forgiving someone every day. But for Jesus our tendencies to persist in and nourish resentment of others fall into the same category as murdering, stealing, or telling lies in court.

In summary, the king's anger, his requirement to show mercy and to forgive from the heart, his condemnation to endless torture for the evil of not forgiving—all of these are intended to open our eyes to the danger that should really worry us. More than anything else, our failure to pass on God's blessing of forgiveness to those who harm us should terrorize our days.

CHAPTER FOUR
God Chasing after Us to Bless Us

*B*iblical hospitality is the prodigal bestowal of blessings by a host upon a guest. The fundamentals of its practice highlight the dignity that God gives to all human beings as well as the divine preoccupation with their well-being. Examining a few texts that display this sacred custom provides another opportunity to explore the joint divine and human effort involved in being a blessing for others.[1]

In the biblical world, hospitality was such a widespread custom because no individual could survive alone. Whether in the parched wilderness or in a more populated area, a person must either belong to a group or die. This reality is what provokes Cain's lament in Genesis 4:10–14 that his punishment of severance from his family is too much for him to bear. Why? Because the curse that he must live as a "fugitive and a wanderer on the earth" (Gen 4:12) means that anyone who meets him may kill him. Travelers in general suffered this fear, and sought out friendly, powerful hosts to provide for them safe havens of rest on their journeys.

There is no single biblical Hebrew word for hospitality, but numerous texts display its practice. Many of these have their origin in the nomadic environment where inns and public sources of food and drinking water were few and far between. Yet it was that very harshness that inspired hosts to provide so generously for the needs of others, since they never knew when they might find themselves in unfamiliar places, suddenly alone and dependent upon the gracious welcome of strangers.

Psalm 23 speaks to us of divine hospitality. Its human manifestation is brought to life in the story of Abraham and Sarah in Genesis 18:1–15.[2]

"The Lord is my shepherd; I shall not want."

Psalm 23 presents one of the most memorable examples of divine hospitality in the Bible. Artists and composers have for centuries celebrated the comforting scenes so simply sketched by this poet, known to us merely as "the psalmist." In Bibles, the psalm is often called a psalm of trust or confidence. But since *real* trust and confidence always emerge from the threat of their opposites, scholars now suggest that the speaker is probably an anxious refugee, creating these reassuring scenes so as to recapture his earlier confidence that God will always provide.

God as Shepherd, God as Sheik

To accomplish this, the psalmist chooses two different images of God. The first, which appears in Psalm 23:1–4, is of God as a shepherd. Although art tends to portray the shepherd as the poor but noble custodian of his few meek animals, the shepherd in the biblical world provided one of the main images and titles for powerful kings and rulers. It was the responsibility of the ruler to provide justice in his realm, especially for those who without him would lack both power and advocacy. Continuing this imagery, the rod and staff (23:4) evoke the real shepherd's club and crook as well as the emblems of the figurative shepherd's kingly rule and office. In Psalm 23, the thought of the Lord's rod and staff—that is, of divine governance and control of all things—gives the psalmist courage in imminent danger; the strength, if so required, to enter into the "darkest valley" (23:4). As so often in the psalms, the danger is not further specified and thus the prayer becomes more fully that of the reader, the one who prays the psalm, seeing the foreboding of that dread dark valley of one's own current peril.

The psalm's second image of God—that of a wealthy, powerful bedouin sheik, the gracious host who takes in and lavishes exaggerated hospitality on the refugee—reinforces the sense of confidence in God, the shepherd-king. The host in Psalm 23:5-6, even within sight of the refugee's enemies, spreads a sumptuous banquet and anoints his head with oil.

The Enemies

Who are these enemies? In the psalms, they represent any encroachment of the realm of death into the land of the living. The most common enemies in the psalms are illness that threatens life, aggressive foreign nations that threaten freedom, and personal rivals who threaten the psalmist's reputation.

Such "enemies" diminish one's capacity to live life in its fullness. Without warning, illness makes it impossible to engage in planned events, no matter how much they are anticipated or how important they are thought to be. National enemies not only restrict a people's freedom, they make even survival questionable. What clearer example is there of the encroachment of death into the land of the living than the horror of war? Likewise, lies, slander, innuendo, and partial truths all damage a person's reputation and decrease or inhibit one's capacity to act effectively.

The psalmist's fight can also be against the enemies within. Feelings of uncontrolled anxiety, fear, envy, lethargy, failure, or diminished value can so narrow one's view of reality as to make life barely bearable. As trust in

God's protection fades, so too does hope and one's vision of what is possible.

In the presence of all these enemies, God sets a bounteous table for the psalmist, as if to say, "Forget all that obscures your view of my plans for your safety and happiness. Enjoy the feast of blessings that I, this very moment, am setting before you. Think about my pact to protect you and my unsurpassed power to do so." The seriousness of this aspect of hospitality, this lavish feasting, is brought out in rabbinic discussions on the host's responsibility to protect a guest. The greater the feast, the greater the responsibility, since one conclusion was that the host had to protect them as the guest until all the food eaten had passed through the system. Their estimates ranged from thirty-six hours to three days. More hospitality implies more responsibility.

Anointing with Oil

The food, however, is not all there is to the abundance of the divine hospitality. At the banquet, God the host anoints the refugee's head with oil. Contemporary readers may pass over this gesture, never realizing the depth of benevolence it reveals. In the biblical world, oil is a staple of daily life. It provides light, warmth, and heat for cooking, and without it, one can hardly live at all in that arid climate.

I had a memorable experience of this during the year that I lived in the holy land. I lived in a house where we had an Arab cook. For both Christmas and Easter, he prepared a lamb that had been roasted and served on a bed of sliced, fried potatoes that swam in the deep moat of the lamb's drippings. Another American woman and I had joined the household in the fall. When the lamb and potatoes were served that Christmas, we both picked the potatoes from the top of the pile, the ones less saturated with fat. Then came Easter and, to our mutual surprise, we noticed that we were digging down for the greasier ones. The reason? By now, our bodies needed the oil that had been leached from them by the Jerusalem climate.

Oil in the biblical world is also used to anoint kings. This gesture symbolizes the elevated status and dignity of the king that flow from his being God's representative on earth. Accordingly, in Psalm 23, the host's anointing of the apparently hapless refugee reveals the reality of this needy person's exalted status and dignity in the eyes of God.

"My cup overflows," the psalmist says, adding one more stroke to his portrait of the bountiful banquet, the image of a host who splashes still more wine into one's barely sipped cup. Costs, or the fear of "running out," are never divine concerns. And do not forget that, like the other signs of God's prodigality, this one too takes place in the sight of the enemies.

God Chases After Us to Do Good for Us

Wonderful as all this is, it is the last verse of Psalm 23 that is the most poignant and touching reminder of God's constant attention as blessing. It claims with certainty that God's goodness (*tob*) and covenant-loyalty (*chesed*) will chase after us all the days of our life. This declaration refers to the host's duty to accompany departing guests and offer them his protection on the first stage of their journey.[3]

The Hebrew *tob* and *chesed* are the manifestations of God's presence. *Tob*, sometimes translated as "rain," conveys essential and vital "goodness" that is required to bring forth life. *Chesed* is a term that is practically impossible to translate into English. We do not have any word that captures its full import in the biblical world. Though it is often translated by "kindness," "loving-kindness," or "steadfast love," *chesed* denotes God's covenant-loyalty or unconditional faithfulness to those who enter into a divine pact. The New Testament Greek translated the Hebrew *chesed* by *charis* or "grace," from which the English word charity is derived. Both *chesed* and *charis* signify that blessing flows from God's unconditional, divine dedication to human beings.

In Psalm 23:6, to say that these personified divine attributes "chase after" the departing guests is to say that God does so. Again, a look at the Hebrew illuminates a startling aspect of this scene. The Hebrew verb *radaph* has been translated traditionally in Psalm 23 as "follow," a placid rendering of a word that so often in other instances in the Bible is translated as "chase after," expressing an eager, tenacious pursuit. It is also frequently used to describe the action of chasing down one's enemies, or being chased down by them.[4] The use of *radaph* in the psalm offers us the vision of a God who extends his blessings with eager and unwavering enthusiasm.

God Shepherds Others through Us

This touching picture of divine blessing as hospitality provides a biblical model of one way to be a blessing for others. Like the shepherd, we can do our part to see that the people whom we encounter during our day lack nothing of God's goodness that is within our power to provide. Perhaps we can offer something as simple as a quiet space or a presence that accords them a moment of stillness and peace in the midst of their normal preoccupations and anxieties. Or maybe we can offer some degree of "protection" to those who, due to their own circumstances, are less fortunate and in a weaker position than we are.

For example, we could shield the very young and the very old from those who seek to take advantage of or abuse them. Or we could welcome the many refugees, migrants, and foreigners in our land who, like the psalmist in Psalm 23, could use the reprieve of hospitality. Those who do not speak fluently the language of a new land are always at a disadvantage. Many never quite understand everything that is being said to them, or have the false certitude that they are saying what they intend to say. Unacquainted with the customs of a foreign place, they use gestures familiar to them to emphasize or replace the spoken word, gestures that may very well convey the opposite of what they mean in their homeland. The very young, the very old, the strangers in a foreign land—all of these are pursued in a special way by the Shepherd. This chasing after them can be manifested through us as we engage them and through our actions as we pass on divine blessings to them.

This pursuit of people in order to do good for them is one of the basic activities of Jesus in the gospels. In particular, he seeks out sinners, tax collectors, and prostitutes, persons whom some have judged and marginalized, perhaps even prayed for, but whom they never actually engage. Jesus, in contrast, spends so much time with these people that, according to Luke, he becomes known as "the friend of sinners" (Luke 7:34), an unlikely reputation unless he hung out with them on a regular basis. In his actions, Jesus incarnates *tob* and *chesed* and makes visible and tangible the reality of God's eager pursuit of people in order to bless them.

Divine Hospitality in Human Trappings (Gen 18:1–15)

Human imitation of the divine hospitality of Psalm 23 is not merely challenging, it is a fearful undertaking. It can be so frightening, in fact, that many never take up the challenge. The story of Abraham's courageous hospitality to three strangers in Genesis 18:1–15 provides a vivid example of what is involved, on the human level, in carrying out this sacred charge to honor strangers and to be a blessing for them.

The opening verse of the narrative sets the scene and provides clues essential for comprehending what follows. In Genesis 18:1 God appears to Abraham as the ancestor sits in the entrance of his tent at the hottest period of the day. What a bad time for visitors to arrive at the home of an elderly couple! While Abraham is nearing the hundred-year mark, Sarah is at least ninety. No wonder he is seated at the entrance of his tent. It is the one place there is likely to be a breeze, just where the blazing hot outside air reacts with the lower temperature of the shade inside the tent.

Poor Abraham! He probably plans to spend the rest of the day doing as little as possible, at least until the weather cools down. But there comes a moment when he lifts up his eyes to survey his arid world and suddenly sees "three men" standing before him. The reader is already clued in that God is among the three. Abraham, not yet recognizing the divine status of the visitors, sees only "men." This fact makes his response even more unexpected, more unnatural.

Abraham and Sarah "Go" (Gen 18:1–8)

As soon as old Abraham sees the men, he runs "from the entrance of his tent" to engage them, and bows down before them. He hurries once again to obey the divine command, "Go." With no sign of hesitation, he leaves behind the familiar security of his dwelling and his plan for the day and rushes into the unknown. He neither stops to ponder who these strangers might be, nor interrogates them about where they are coming from and where they are going. He thinks only of offering them hospitality.[5] Foremost in his mind, it seems, is the urgency of somehow being a blessing for them. The three-fold repetition of "hurry" in the following verses shows that this haste characterizes all of the couple's preparations for their unexpected guests.

Abraham's bow to the strangers is the common Mid-Eastern gesture of respect in social exchanges.[6] It also shows the strangers that Abraham considers them more important than he is. He accepts them as "lords" and makes himself their "servant." However, in Genesis 18, this convention is more than mere Mid-Eastern politesse. Old Abraham's bow recognizes the human dignity of the visitors. They are worthy of special attention, if for no other reason than that they are images and likenesses of God. In them, God comes into the old couple's life.

This suggestion is further strengthened by the one reason Abraham puts forth for his invitation. According to Genesis 18:5, he welcomes the strangers simply because they happened to have come upon him. As far as he knows when they first arrive, he has never met them before. They are not friends, nor allies, nor people to whom he owes favors.

Abraham's offer of a "little water" and a "little bread" is in the end far more than that. He and Sarah offer the very best they have and that in abundance. They lay out their own banquet, their own version of the plenty of the sheik's table in Psalm 23. Abraham's bread is not simply the bit that is ready at hand. His morsel is no mere pittance. Rather, it turns out to be more fresh rolls than three men are able to eat.

The unnatural human effort put into their hospitality is evident in the details of the making of that bread. Abraham tells Sarah to "hurry" and to use not the regular but the "choice flour" for it. This was the flour that took much labor to grind and regrind. This was the fully refined flour that was prepared for feasts.

While Sarah is busy kneading rolls, Abraham runs to his herd where he personally selects a "calf, tender and good"—the Hebrew word for good is *tob*—and gives it to his servant who "hastened" to prepare it. Remember that for the people of Abraham's world meat was not the daily fare. It was a luxury. Bread, goat cheese, and a few vegetables were enough for their meals. Meat was reserved for the greatest of family celebrations, for births and weddings.

Luke 15's breaking of this routine of modest meals is what makes the prodigal father's slaughter of the "fatted calf" upon the return of his spendthrift son so maddening to that son's older brother. The calf marks the younger son's return as something to celebrate. Likewise, Abraham's serving of the calf marks the presence of the strangers at his tent as an event that is worthy of celebration. As the scene closes, we see that old Abraham does not even partake of the splendid outlay with his guests, but *stands* in attendance on them.

In summary, in the hospitality of Genesis 18:1–8, Abraham and Sarah are a blessing to apparent strangers. Their prodigality manifests the biblical conviction that the divine supply of gifts, which God showers constantly on humans, is endless. Those who pass on these blessings to others insert themselves into the providential stream of blessings that flows freely and without ceasing from the divine into the human dimension of life.

Going Leads to a New Adventure (Gen 18:9–15)

But the narrative does not end with the hospitality scene. The passage continues to reveal the consequences of the old couple's hurry into the unknown. Their lavish hospitality leads to one of the biggest surprises of their long life together, the gift of the son for whom they had given up all hope.

Genesis 18:9–15 reinforces the commonplace that God is never outdone in generosity. Scholars frequently note that this text employs the literary motif of people entertaining gods unawares and being divinely rewarded for doing so. In our text, the visitors whose divine identity is slowly unfolded—they know such things as Sarah's name and her inner thoughts and that she laughed to herself—announce that the birth of the long-awaited son will occur within the year. At ninety years of age, the barren Sarah gives a hearty laugh at this announcement (the name Isaac is derived from the Hebrew root meaning "laugh"). But she will indeed have a son within the year, and Abraham will be on the way finally to becoming that "great nation" that God promised him when he left everything and took that long-ago first step of his journey into the unknown.

Genesis 18, like so many biblical texts, shows how an ordinary encounter becomes a place where the invisible

God is revealed. To allow God to act in us, and thus manifest the union of heaven and earth that is every human being, requires that we move out of our lethargy, that we veer from our beaten path, and that we allow God to lead us into new terrain. To "go" into the lives of others is scary, filled as it is with the unfamiliar. To refuse to go, however, blocks what could be the greatest adventure that God plans for us before it has a chance to begin.

One antidote for our qualms is to have the command to "Be a blessing" writ so large upon the tablet of our consciousness that it dwarfs little notes of uncertainty and anxiety before they swell to a booming chorus that paralyzes our mind, chills our heart, and hurries us back into the cave of our tiny, stagnant, but oh-so-secure "life." Only great faith, like that of Abraham and Sarah, can embolden us to sing a new song, God's song, whose melody is blessing and whose theater is the entire universe.

CHAPTER FIVE
The Extravagance of Divine Blessings

God's blessings are not merely abundant. They are extravagant, beyond all expectation and imagining. The greatest divine extravagance is the gift of human life. Only human beings can imagine and participate with God in blessing others and the world. Only humans are capable of seeing a divine vision that would replace human calculation for personal gain with outrageous generosity that is bent on bettering the lives of others. Deuteronomy 6:10–19 and Matthew 20:1–16 teach that personal experience of God's exaggerated giving introduces us to the concept and prepares us to pass it on to others.

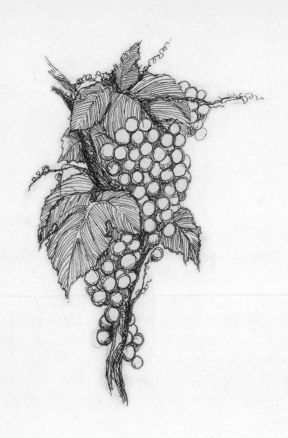

The Enjoyment of Blessings for Which We Do Not Labor

The covenant blessings are conveyed in Deuteronomy 6:10–19 as features of the land that God will give the people, the land that God promised to show to Abraham once he had left his homeland and set out to be a blessing for others. The extravagance of the blessings is shown by their magnitude and by the fact that they are free. God will give Israel splendid cities that they did not build, houses full of goods of all sorts that they did not provide, cisterns that they did not dig, and thriving vineyards and olive groves that they did not plant. All of these normally require formidable labor and time.

Everyone who is responsible for others can appreciate the effort of setting up a household. Imagine what it must have been like in the biblical world. Most things were handmade by the owner or gained through barter of items produced by painstaking and protracted human effort. Houses had a cooking oven, provided the owner made one. Cooking pots, storage jars, and lamps had to be shaped and fired from clay. Furniture—chests, tables, chair frames—was all made by hand. And God promised to supply it all!

And then there were the cisterns. We may not naturally consider cisterns a blessing. But they were. They were required to store water, essential in a land that has only two seasons, the rainy period and the drought. Cisterns were also used to store wine and oil. In a world without dynamite or power tools, they were laboriously chipped out of rock with pick-axes, and then plastered to prevent leakage into the marl layers found in rocky terrain.

In the land God will give Israel, they will also find mature vineyards and olive groves that they did not plant. Isaiah 5:1–7 depicts the effort involved in bringing these agricultural blessings to a state where they produce usable harvests, as it describes how God (the vineyard owner) settles Israel (the vineyard) in the promised land.

Though situated "on a very fertile hill," the owner must spade the piece of land and clear it of stones. These stones are often stacked to construct the vineyard's wall. Then the owner plants the choicest of vines, all carefully chosen. Like the shepherd who knows each sheep by name, the vintner knows the needs and weaknesses of each vine and carefully cultivates it. To Isaiah's description, John 15 adds the detail that the owner prunes the vine so that the little water it gets from the dew will not be wasted on shoots that are too fragile to produce fruit.

In addition to hewing out a cistern and a wine-press, the vineyard owner builds a watchtower. Since grapes mature and are gathered during the hottest time of the year, in September toward the end of the dry season, their juice and sweetness proffer an almost irresistible temptation to every passer-by. To protect their investment, the owner and his family would move into this watchtower at harvest time.

Like the vineyard, the olive groves that God will give the people in the land will already be producing usable olives. The incredible wonder of this gift lies in the fact that it takes seven years for these trees to start bearing fruit, and fifteen to twenty years for them to reach maturity. Given the vital role of olive oil in the daily life of people in biblical times, the gift of mature trees is like that of a dependable, thriving business or livelihood.

By extension, the contemporary parallels of these blessings would include any divine gift that humans enjoy, but for which they did not work. Perhaps the most common—and commonly taken-for-granted—gift is the home that parents provide for their children. To be born of responsible and caring parents, those who have already done the hard work of maturing into decent adults, is one of the greatest of divine blessings. For those who have been so blessed, their childhood years are a school for learning the exaggerated quality of God's attentiveness to and delight in them.

When the Fruits of Our Labor Go to Others

Human life also provides experiences of the other side of the coin of divine blessing. While we like the idea of enjoying the fruits of the labor of others, we are often not so content to see others enjoying the fruits of *our* labor. There are many who, after working hard for years raising children, or developing a system, project, or business, see the benefits (and rewards) of their efforts go to people who do not, by human standards, deserve them—to the fool, the stranger, or the sinner. Parents, who lay down every moment of their lives for their children for decades, sometimes reap little in return. Employees may be downsized upon the completion of a project and see their work go to another who seems incapable of appreciating its value, who changes it for the sake of change, and who ultimately trashes it.

The biblical author Ecclesiastes makes a typically acerbic observation on such scenarios: "I hated all my toil in which I had toiled under the sun, seeing that I must leave it to those who come after me—and who knows whether they will be wise or foolish? Yet they will be master of all for which I toiled and used my wisdom under the sun. This also is vanity" (Eccl 2:18–19).

To what wisdom is Ecclesiastes finally led by such honest pondering? He concludes that God is in control of everything that life brings, and that mortals often *cannot* understand what God is doing. In 6:12 Ecclesiastes says, "For who knows what is good for mortals while they live the few days of their vain life, which they pass like a shadow?" The only thing for humans to do is to discard narrow, learned, or imbibed views of what ideally *should* be, and of how people ideally *should* act, and of what will make them happy, and instead be content with *what is* and trust that it plays some role in God's plan to bless.

The book of Ecclesiastes itself is a great blessing because it addresses fundamental questions of many faith-filled adults, people who look at life with eyes wide open and with doubts that they are afraid to voice. They do not wish to appear disloyal to God. They do not, like Ecclesiastes, honestly describe the reality around them, or like Jacob at the Jabbok, stand their ground and fight with

God. In effect, they fail to persevere in their quest for understanding of their covenant partner.

One of Marian Wright Edelman's "Lessons for Life" provides a larger picture, which takes into consideration the passages from both Deuteronomy and Ecclesiastes. She writes,

> *Be a good ancestor. Stand for something bigger than yourself. Add value to the Earth during your sojourn.* Give something back. Every minute you drink from wells you did not dig, are sheltered by builders you will never know, are protected by police and soldiers and neighbors and caretakers whose names are in no record books, are tended by healing hands of every hue and heritage, and are fed and clothed by the labors of countless others. Olive Schreiner, the South African writer, said: "Where I lie down worn out, other men will stay young and fresh. By the steps I have cut they will climb; by the stairs that I have built they will mount. They may never know the name of the man (or woman) who made them. At the clumsy work they will laugh; when the stones roll they will curse me. But they will mount, and on my work, they will climb, and by my stair...And no man liveth to himself, and no man dies to himself." What will

your obituary say? What will your legacy in life be?[1]

The Covenant Context of Blessing

A word remains to be said about Deuteronomy's covenant context, one of the main analogies used in the Bible to convey the gift of the great divine-human project of life.

Though not all biblical covenants are conditional, this is the case with that found in Deuteronomy. For many, this realization reduces the gift of a relationship with God to keeping a burdensome list of rules (which, in fact, obscures its main purpose). A conditional covenant works this way: if humans (the vassals) keep the rules, they will be blessed by God (the covenant lord) and if they break the rules, their Lord will punish them. Many biblical texts do indeed claim that accountability and retribution are aspects of the covenant relationship. For example, Deuteronomy 28 sets out a series of blessings for faithful vassals and curses for unfaithful ones.

But many people, including many biblical writers, find this too-narrow a view of the divinely initiated pact between God and Israel. They fear it leaves unanswered the honest questions of adults whose faith seeks understanding. For example: What is so divine, so Godlike, about keeping rules in order to receive gifts and avoid punishment? Is this not already the approach to life by which most of us are taught to operate? Moreover, why would one want to endure such a covenant in the first place? Why not seek freedom from such a burden and so escape the terror and stress it engenders? In short, why bother at all with a covenant relationship with God?

The Covenant Reveals That God Cannot Bear to Be Apart from Us

Many biblical texts that address these questions would persuade us that the covenant is not an ultimatum from an overbearing ruler, but rather evidence that God cannot bear to be apart from us, or even to be out of communication, experienced as blessing, with us. These texts show that God so much desires a relationship with mortals that, though we seem inherently incapable of fidelity, God will nevertheless be loyal to us. This covenant—which is not annulled when the human party breaks it—reveals the divine desire to be with human beings unconditionally and to bless them constantly.

The Bible makes it abundantly clear that if the covenant did function on an objective merit basis, no one could possibly keep it. Like people everywhere, the Israelites (and later, Jesus' disciples) are *in themselves* incapable of perfect fidelity. They cannot keep all the rules, nor can they consistently image God perfectly. As Paul writes, "For I do not do the good I want, but the evil I do not want is what I do" (Rom 7:19).

The prophet Hosea illustrates how a conditional covenant can reveal the unconditional loyalty of God by the way he depicts God's quandary about how to deal with the Israelites when they break the covenant (Hos 11:1–9). Objectively, Israel should be completely annihilated for its infidelities. But God cannot carry out the punishment and end their relationship.

In his review of their history together, Hosea begins with God loving them and calling them out of Egypt; their response to this liberation is to worship other gods (Hos 11:1–2). Such a covenant breach demands judgment and accordingly God announces their fall to the Assyrians (Hos 11:5–6).

However, with this common, unexamined view of how the covenant works, Hosea intertwines verses that show the other side of the divine dilemma by portraying God as a tender, loving parent. Hosea 11:3–4 reads, "Yet it was I who taught Ephraim [Israel] to walk, I took them up in my arms; but they did not know that I healed them. I led them with cords of human kindness, with bands of love. I was to them like those who lift infants to their cheeks."

Ultimately, divine compassion tempers divine judgment. "How can I give you up, Ephraim? How can I hand you over, O Israel? How can I make you like Admah? How can I treat you like Zeboiim [two cities destroyed with Sodom and Gemorrah]? My heart recoils within me; my compassion grows warm and tender. I will not execute my fierce anger; I will not again destroy Ephraim; *for I am God and no mortal*, the Holy One in your midst" (Hos 11:8–9).

How different God is from us! We operate with the Greek notion of justice, which is often conveyed by a blindfolded woman who holds a scale in each hand and metes out the exact punishment deserved for the crime committed. In contrast, God's judgment is tempered with mercy.

As Hosea claims, God does not follow strictly the conditional covenant stipulations. Israel is not cursed and destroyed. They were conquered by Assyria in 721 BC, but not annihilated. Like Hosea, who could not bring himself to divorce his wife, even though she was repeatedly unfaithful to him (he loved her too much), neither can God cast off Israel because it too fails to be faithful. For God, maintaining the relationship with human beings is apparently more important than retribution, than going strictly by a set of rules.

God's unconditional loyalty forces us to realize that covenant commandments are more than a set of criteria by which we are judged. Their profound purpose is to teach us more about God and to change our behavior. Just as by adopting the views, mannerisms, and turns of phrase of our companions, we become more like them, by putting the covenant provisions into practice, we become more faithful icons of God in whose likeness we are created.

Participation in the covenant relationship with God and the reception of the greatest divine gifts require action. Deuteronomy enjoins the Israelites to "*do* what is right [*yashar*] and good [*tob*]" (Deut 6:18) so that they can enter the promised land. In the Bible, knowledge of God comes from having experiences with God. Likewise, St. Gregory of Nyssa taught that the best way to learn about God is to do what God does.

Led by the Rules of the Covenant into the Unknown

Allowing the Hebrew covenant and the teachings of Jesus to form us into more authentic images of God takes us into new territory, new situations, which we might not otherwise choose to enter. Perhaps this is simply because they are unfamiliar to us, or because they involve more effort than we are willing to make, or more risk than we are accustomed to take. Doing things that are right and good, like following Jesus, takes more energy and creates more stress than merely refraining from clearly heinous acts like thievery, adultery, and murder.

Doing good gets us into more than we bargain for. Deuteronomy 22:1–3 provides one entertaining illustration of a possible scenario:

> You shall not watch your neighbor's ox or sheep straying away and ignore them; you shall take them back to their owner. If the owner does not reside near you or you do not know who the owner is, you shall bring it to your own house, and it shall remain with you until the owner claims it; then you shall return it. You shall do the same with a neighbor's donkey; you shall do the same with a neighbor's garment; and you shall do the same with *anything* else that your neighbor loses and you find. You *may not* withhold your help.

You can almost imagine lovers of God just hoping they will see no lost belongings, for all the trouble it will cost them. "Oh, no! Not another dumb ox..." But the truth is that God cares enough to think of such things; and wants us to do the same. Good deeds are costly. Imagine the expense and trouble of feeding an ox for a single day! And perhaps the one who finds this big ox has no experience in handling animals. The application of the behavior to "anything" that someone loses and that we find really seems to go too far. I mean, some people are just careless, right? Why should we look after their property? The answer is simple: because God, who has the larger view, would have us do so.

The Gifts May Have to "Go"

To take care of someone else's ox or donkey will require that some of the gifts we have received from God "go." This is often the case when we do what is right and good. Yet the truth is that the gifts we have were given to us for the purpose of passing them on, of making it possible for us to be a blessing to those who are less fortunate than us. No matter how "poor" we are, we can still give gifts like friendship, empathy, affirmation, forgiveness, and presence.

Imagine what each day would be like if we tried to outdo God in generosity, to pass on more blessings to others than God bestows on us, to give more of our time, energy, and precious belongings than we ever thought imaginable.

What prevents us from taking up this challenge? Fear, I should say. We are afraid to let our blessings "go" because we sincerely believe that God has allotted us a certain number of blessings, most of which are received by the time we are forty or fifty or sixty years old. We think that if we give away too much of what we have, we will not have enough left to live peacefully and securely in our last years. Though the Bible claims that God's blessings never run out, we so often live with the conviction that they will. In times like these, texts like Lamentations 3:22-23 remind us: "The steadfast love [chesed] of the Lord never ceases, his mercies never come to an end; they are new every morning; great is your faithfulness."

The fear that there is a limit to God's gifts should alert us that we are following false gods. It also keeps us enslaved to them in the form of things that we think can provide the security we are so afraid of losing. We continue in bondage to money, to people who appear to be powerful in circumstances that matter to us, to the commonplace attitudes of most people. And in the meantime, the contemporary equivalents of the wonderful features of the land that God promises to give to Israel—those splendid cities with cisterns and furnished houses, producing vineyards and olive groves—elude us, and those to whom God would have us pass them on. Once again, we miss the great adventure of being a blessing for all the peoples of the earth. We slip out of the mainstream of divine giving and instead drift aimlessly on the sidelines of life.

CHAPTER SIX
When Blessing Provokes Evil

A well-known parable compares the kingdom of heaven to a landowner who hires and pays day laborers. The hiring is described in Matthew 20:1–7, and the payment in 20:8–16. The landowner goes out "together with the early morning" to hire workers and send them into his vineyard (the Greek verb for send is 'apostellein from which "apostle" is derived). The landowner agrees to pay to each the usual daily wage, a denarius. This routine still goes on in peaceful times today; for example, at the Arab bus station across the road from Damascus Gate. Villagers come in from the area around Jerusalem and wait to be hired.

In the parable, the owner goes out four more times throughout the day to hire additional laborers. He agrees to pay "whatever is just" to those whom he hires at nine a.m., and apparently the same amount to those whom he hires at noon and 3:00 p.m. When he goes at 5:00 p.m., he finds others "standing around" the market place. When he asks why they stand idle the whole day, they claim it is because no one has hired them. Their words don't ring quite true. Where were they the last four times he came to look for laborers? Isn't their conduct a little suspect? A little less than industrious? Not quite edifying? No matter...the owner sends them to the vineyard. At evening, the master sends the steward to assemble the workers and to pay first those who arrived last. To each a denarius. This is surprising, but the real shock occurs when the last are paid the same as the first. The payment jars us. It provokes our thought, perhaps our concern.

We can understand the dissatisfaction of the first workers with the landowner's apparent arbitrariness and discrimination.[1] Almost all of us are naturally upset when, for example, we lose out on something that we deserve because an employer, a superior, or a parent acts arbitrarily or shows favoritism for another. And so we readily empathize with the first workers. Is not their claim a just one?

Context of the Parable in Matthew

The evangelist Matthew situates this parable in the context of Jesus' journey to Jerusalem and his teachings on discipleship. By means of a series of "reversals" of the hearer's expectations,[2] Jesus addresses the all-too-frequent seeming disparity between divine and human expectations. Framing Matthew's parable are versions of the warning that, at the final judgment, the last will be first and the first last. This axiom is one of the gospels' pithy reminders that God does not see things as we do. In particular, it invites us to consider, once again, how different divine criteria for worthiness are from our own.

The significance of the reversal in Matthew 20 is revealed in the dialogue between the landowner and the first group of workers. Like the unforgiving servant in Matthew 18, the first workers make the assumption, unrecognized but still operating in most members of the Christian community, that hiring and paying in the kingdom of heaven follow the norms of earthly business. The hard words of Jesus to those first workers are intended to open their eyes, and ours as well, to the slavish unexamined assumption that only those who do the same work will receive the same pay from God—the sadly limited assumption of the quid pro quo.

So the first workers assume that they will receive more than the others, but the landowner has a different compensation plan. The workers' complaint in Matthew 20:12 expresses their indignation: "Equal to *us* who have borne the burden of the day and the scorching heat, *them you* have made." This translation preserves the unusual word order of the Greek and helps us to grasp its special emphases.

The accusation sets out the three parties involved in the situation: us, them, and you. These are, after all, the parties involved in every situation where we become resentful at what others receive from God. A closer look at each party draws us more deeply into the parable and helps us appreciate the human difficulty involved in accepting Jesus' divine view.

"Equal to US" (Matt 20:12)

Us refers to the first group of workers. What do they experience as they come forward at last to receive their payment? What was their day like? They got up and out earlier than anyone else. They rushed to find work, were hired by the landowner, and worked the entire day. Then they waited the longest to be paid. They complain that they are the ones who suffered through the scorching heat—no small feat in the biblical world. Those are the hours when many stop to rest, when the sun bakes away all energy, and when work feels all but impossible. But that was when they labored for the owner, even through their own exhaustion.

In Jesus' original parable, these workers possibly voiced the view of his opponents, often religious leaders who challenged Jesus' teachings. They see themselves as the ones who have devoted their entire lives to God's work. They study and are dedicated completely to keeping the covenant laws. But the outlook of some of them has become legalistic, and they project this human view onto God. Worse, they begin to treat God as a landlord, an overseer, the mere owner of a business. Their view of God clashes here, as it often does, with what Jesus teaches and lives.[3] John Donahue notes that "Jesus does not condemn the Pharisees but warns that a desire to live justly according to the covenant should not lead to an attitude that dictates to the covenant-God how mercy and generosity should be shown. The line between following God's will and *deciding what God wills* is always thin and fragile."[4]

For the evangelist, the first workers voice the "pharisaical" views and attitudes of members of today's Christian community who have fallen into the same human patterns of evaluation as those religious leaders of Jesus' day. Because of their tireless dedication, they have come to perceive themselves as a cut above all other Christians. They do, indeed, work hard but this also makes them feel superior to others. As usual, these outlooks clash with the vision of Jesus. They follow, not Jesus, but celebrated human values.

"Equal to us, THEM you have made" *(Matt 20:12)*

*Them...*These are the ones who, from a human point of view, seemingly do not work as God would have them do—the ones not dedicated enough to commit their time fully to the tasks assigned them in the kingdom. In the scorching heat of the day, these are the ones who knock off early, take a little rest, dally, or arrive late to work.

In Jesus' day, *them* represents those who are marginalized by "religious" people because they are less dedicated to the work of the kingdom. In Matthew, these are exemplified by the tax collectors, prostitutes, and sinners. The Pharisees are scandalized because Jesus spends time with these people and even eats with them and extends to them the gift of God's presence, love, and forgiveness (Matt 5:46; 9:10-11; 11:19; 21:31-32). For this outrageous comportment, the Pharisees give Jesus a title that should honor every Christian; namely, "a friend of tax collectors and sinners" (Matt 11:19).

Our familiarity with this habit of Jesus has lessened the shock value of his conduct. We are so used to the idea of Jesus being with "sinners" that we do not grasp the sense of scandal felt by his contemporaries. We need to look again at the tax collectors of Jesus' day if we are to enter more deeply into the parable and recognize the contemporary parallels of these sinners. It will also show us that their despicable deportment is, at some level, no different from our own.

The tax collectors of Jesus' day are infamous for lining their pockets by abusing the power of their office. They are appointed by the Roman rulers or their surrogates to collect a set amount of money for the government. Their own pay will come from whatever they collect beyond that. If they are clever enough, they can become rich off their fellow citizens. Tax collectors are held as no better than robbers and murderers, and their trade is one that religious Jews are exhorted not to take up.[5]

In our day, "tax collectors" would include those who use the powers that come with their office or position to acquire extras for themselves at the expense of those under them. They improve their lives by taking from the less powerful. Some obvious modern day examples of tax collectors include international, national, state, and local officials who use their position to pander to themselves rather than tend to the needs of those whom they are appointed to serve.

Modern day tax collectors need not have great authority. In Jesus' day, even those who collected tolls on the roadways could filch more than the official charge. Anyone with the tiniest bit of power over another—due to age, wealth, background, position—has the potential to act like a tax collector.

No matter how great or how small the abuse, it always engenders the disgust and disdain of those who think themselves above it. There is the all-too-human tendency to judge, to stand aloof from, and to look down upon the offender. The divine tendency—Jesus' tendency—is to seek them out, to spend time with them, even to get the reputation of being their friend. In this parable, Jesus even makes them equal to the first workers.

"Equal to us, them YOU have made" (Matt 20:12)

You represents the landowner, the one with the divine view of payment for work done in the kingdom of heaven. He is the visualization, for Jesus' listeners, of the invisible God who, though always present, is usually forgotten in human interchanges and transactions.

The accusation of the industrious and dedicated workers—"Equal to us, them you have made"—precipitates the clash between the divine and human views. Their criticism is fired by their conviction that divine gifts must be distributed on a tit-for-tat basis. Their view is simple: I work this much; you pay me this much. I do more work than others; you pay me more than you pay them. I fawn and flatter you so much; you reward me proportionately. These industrious and dedicated workers know that life is not often fair. All the more reason, then, that God, at least, should treat everyone in an equal manner, or at least in the manner that *they* would judge to be equal—their tit-for-tat basis.

In Jesus' parable, the first workers (and those of similar attitude) are disappointed when God does not reward them for simply doing their agreed-upon task. They are displeased when God does not give them a treat or a bonus for doing their job. They need special affirmation of their "extra work," expressed by something more than others receive.

A rabbinic parable from about AD 300 provides a version of Matthew 20:1–16, which most of us would understand and even prefer, but which would not provoke us to think, nor to readjust our view of God, nor to follow Jesus more closely. The rabbinic parable concerns a king who hires many day laborers. He notices that one is more industrious than the rest, so after this one has worked for only two hours, the king calls him apart and then walks up and down with him for the rest of the day. When the king pays the industrious worker the same as the rest, he explains that even though this one worked for only two hours, he did in those two hours more work than all the other workers together.[6]

Unlike the rabbinic parable, that of Jesus challenges our human views of God. This is more clearly seen by exploring what the wages really mean. Also, the original Greek reveals more of this challenge.

"Take what is yours and go" (Matt 20:14)

How does the landowner respond to the first workers; and Jesus to us when we complain either inwardly or outwardly about unequal treatment? First the landowner says, "Take what belongs to you and go." What can be so satisfying that people will be content to walk away from "unfair" treatment? In the parable, "What belongs to you" is the agreed-upon wage of one denarius.[7] For Christians, it is the kingdom of God and eternal life.[8] In both cases, the wage is a daily matter, reminiscent of the "daily bread" of Matthew's version of the Our Father. It represents whatever is needed for the day.

Matthew 20 gives a surprising twist to the command, "Go." This time it is not the gifts, but rather the receivers who go. When Jesus' disciples notice apparent irregularities in God's delivery of divine gifts, they are simply to take what they are given, the more-than-adequate and unfathomable gift of the kingdom for that day, and walk on. They are to abandon their quid-pro-quo assumptions and expectations that Jesus will treat them differently because they worked longer or tried harder, and also discard the notion that how and to whom Jesus distributes divine gifts is any of their business. As they venture into new territory, they become aware that even as Jesus gives to others, he remains with them. Wonder replaces anger as they are whirled along a divine vortex of blessings that quickly transports them light years away from their tortuous comparisons with others. These latter fade as another phase of God's delightful plan for their life takes vivid shape before them.

How do we enter this divine vortex? How do we abandon our disgust with Jesus' behavior and stick by his side as he moves on? We can do so by words as simple and honest as these: "Well, I certainly don't get that! And I don't like it. Nevertheless, I'll just take what is mine, and go. The rest is beyond my grasp. I guess I don't need to understand it after all."

"Am I not allowed to do what I choose with what belongs to me?" (Matt 20:5)

Theoretically, most of us would answer Jesus' last question in the affirmative. Emotionally, however, we seldom do so. Few, if any, of us are ever fully willing to grant God absolute freedom, in spite of the irony than none of us can allow or prevent God from doing anything.

In the Greek, "what belongs to me" reads literally "the-my-things" *['en tois 'emois]*, and emphasizes the fact that the payment given is personal. It is something that only Jesus can give. It is his unique possession. No mortals can acquire it by their own efforts. "The-my-things" are the gifts of the kingdom of heaven and of eternal life. Foremost among these is the companionship of God. These are gifts that no mortal can take away. Yet we, like the hardest workers, fail to realize the magnitude of these blessings. Most of the time, we don't even give them a thought.

"Is your eye evil because I, I am good?" (Matt 20:15)

Jesus' final question—"Is *your* eye evil [*ponaeros*] because I, I am good ['*ego 'agathos eími*]?"—is the real shocker of the parable. According to Jan Lambrecht, the verse asks: Are you angry? Are you jealous? Indeed (literally), are you evil, because I am good?[9] Jesus' words condemn the taking of offense at goodness done to others.

His question sets side by side the laborers' evil perspective and Jesus' goodness. This juxtaposition precipitates a shocking thought: that the bestowal of divine goodness may provoke evil in those who witness it. But in truth, it is not God's goodness itself that causes evil. It is just that the brilliance of Jesus' question sheds its light on the workers' challenge to divine justice and thus reveals the masquerade of their and our own poor human concept of justice. Without the truth of divine goodness, human weaknesses can flourish and be reinforced into evils. Without the light that shines on them through the behavior of Jesus' disciples, these evils will continue to masquerade as goodness and justice.

What is truly evil is to project onto God our poor human quid-pro-quo dispensation of divine goodness.

Jesus takes for granted that God gives people what they deserve, and that human beings have not the divine ability to determine what these rewards might be. There is so much that goes on personally between God and every individual that no one else ever knows about. Concerning human indignation at God's beneficence, Jan Lambrecht asks, "How can a person who him- or herself has received gift after gift and mercy upon mercy protest against the Giver because He also gives to others?"[10] John Donahue goes even further: "Not to rejoice in the benefits given others is to cut ourselves off from those benefits we ourselves have received. Our eyes too become evil."[11]

The poignancy of the text is conveyed in the original Greek by a few simple pronouns, summarized here: First, there are "us" whom the employer makes equal to "them." The "us" are told, "Take the-your-things and go." Then, the landowner asks if he is not free to do with "the-my-things" whatever he pleases, reminding us to whom everything really does belong and who has given us all that we have.

Once again, Jesus shocks his hearers into elevating their assumptions to a higher vantage point. From this new perspective, they can see that what they had thought a solid basis for human justice, their own little slice of life, looks different to God because God sees the larger picture. They also see the fallacy of their principle that what people receive should be in direct proportion to their industry. That path—so wide and well-beaten and easy to follow—has been mapped out for us by those whom Jesus sees as "evil."

Granted that God is good and that this is somehow conveyed or in the background of every biblical passage, what is the particular expression of divine goodness (*'agathos*) in this parable? On one level, it is God keeping the covenant-promise of daily gifts. It is also the giving of a full day's wage to those who do not earn it. This latter reveals the divine quality of God's giving, which by human standards seems exaggerated, even misplaced. God gives too much to those who do so little.

This is really the case with most of us. In fact, Lambrecht suggests that all Christians are "workers of the eleventh hour."[12] We only think that, like the first workers, we have worked the longest and the hardest because we do not and cannot know completely the struggles of those around us. Only God can appreciate those.

Who are the people who, in fact, bear the burden of the day in the scorching heat, who never for a moment are allowed to lay down the burden of their mental and physical sufferings? They could be political prisoners who suffer unimaginable torture and humiliation, who suffer alone, forgotten except by the people who love them the most. Some of these are not even granted a public execution, which at least would make their death a noble testimony to justice, truth, and love and could be witnessed and marveled at by many. Indeed, they would be honored as martyrs.

Or those who bear the burden of the day and its scorching heat may be those who suffer terminal illnesses, whose days are bound by an unrelieved chain of pain. Others are oppressed from birth and live without hope of freedom. Still others suffer the mental anguish of old memories or the frustrations of chemical imbalances, inescapable since they are built into every cell of their bodies.

When we line up beside such sufferings all the gifts that we enjoy daily, we cannot deny our capacity for evil. But this recognition can also give us the courage to risk living with the conviction that every time we let go of our emotional reactions to apparent inequalities, we are setting ourselves up for more amazing adventures with our good Lord.

Fear of Accepting Divine Blessings

No human being is ever alone. We are joined from birth with the living God who made us and who cannot bear to be separated from us. In other words, nothing—no person, disease, tragedy, or even joy—can ever get between us and God. It is impossible. Every breath we draw reminds us of just how close we are. Psalm 73:23 puts it this way: "I am continually with you; you hold my right hand." In the final words of the Gospel of Matthew, Jesus says, "And remember, I am with you always, to the end of the age."

In the Bible, to "remember" means "to do something about." It is far more than recalling a piece of information. For example, God remembers the barren Rachel and she bears Joseph (Gen 30:22). And the frequent cry in the psalms, "Remember me," begs the covenant God to *do something* about the psalmists' situation or praises God for an action taken on their behalf (Pss 25:6; 74:2; 74:18, 22; 89:47, 50; 98:3; etc.).

Like remembering, being a blessing requires *action*. We must "go" and going usually entails change. I have a delightful friend who opened my eyes to a refreshing way of doing this by his use of the opener, "I decided to surprise myself and..." One never knows what he might do! The phrase itself provokes many possibilities. One could give up meat after a tenth annual physical recommends this, or refrain from a habitual response or a knee-jerk reaction and replace it with one that is completely "out of character."

Another change that most of us could make would be to slow down and truly engage or merge with people we encounter in our daily routine. For example, I do not enjoy grocery shopping and try to finish this indispensable chore as quickly as possible. But people in traffic are oblivious to my needs. They do not drive as I wish them to. They accelerate too slowly, and they do not seem to know where they are going, what lane to be in, where to turn, or that a green light means *move* and that intersections are not parking lots. To put it briefly, they are in my way.

Once I arrive in the store, *more* humans are in my way. They cannot decide what they want; they block the produce with their carts; they pore over arrays of pasta as if their life depended on passing an exam on the nutritional value of each; they chat with the checker whom, unfortunately for me, they know personally. They help bag their groceries and *then* start digging for their money—the exact change, of course, down to the penny—or worse, they write a check. When my turn finally comes, I'm ready to treat the checker like a cheap robot, sigh my way through the ordeal, and at last drag myself from the store and out into the traffic where, once again, only I seem to know how to drive.

All of this flows from the grand, unbounded store of empathy that I stockpile for myself. But it blocks the flow of God's compassion in me for others and the divine desire to bless them through me. Occasionally, I manage to walk out my door with the view that grocery shopping is a mission to be a blessing to others. What a different experience it becomes when I surprise myself and let others go first; when I try to understand what is going on in them from how they drive, stand, and move; when I peacefully and at first silently engage them (as opposed to blurting out some mindless commonplace as if I'd pushed a button on an answering machine); when, in short, I respect and honor them as the presence and companionship of God, whom they embody.

My habitual grocery-shopping behavior also prevents me from appreciating the blessing that being able to buy food, and such an assortment of food, is. Other people did all the work required to produce it, and many of them will never benefit from their efforts. But I do—and I would not want them to consider me Ecclesiastes' fool.

Just as God first loves us, God first surprises us with outrageously extravagant gifts and thus inspires us to imitation. One of my most recent experiences of distinctively divine prodigality happened one Christmas. For a present, some friends, a mentor and his wife, took me to a genuine Irish boutique and invited me to pick out *whatever* I wanted! The store was filled with wonderful things, which, like my friends, were not cheap. It carried uniquely crafted pieces of jewelry and handwoven suits of beautifully dyed wool. More remarkable to me than all of these was the certainty that my friends meant what they said and were thrilled to give me such a gift.

Another example of outrageous blessing is a Native American woman who was called "Woman who gives everything away." She was given this name at her baptism because that was the image of God she revealed to her community. Whenever people came to her home and admired something, she did not let them leave without it. (Her children did draw the line however, when someone admired their baby-grand piano!)

The best way to learn to be a blessing is to practice divine prodigality. The unforgettable Christmas gift and the existence of "Woman who gives everything away" inspire us and give us a glimpse of divine openhandedness. For another inkling, we could try, for a day or even for a single moment, to outdo God's giving, to be preposterously extravagant gift-givers, even to "misplace" our generosity simply to surprise ourselves and to taste the kind of experience that God intends humans to thrive on.

Living a Human Life Is Not for the Timid

This adventure of living a *human* life with God as our Partner in blessing is not for the timid. It requires the courage and tenacious energy of Jacob, which enabled him to hold onto his divine attacker until he blessed him; and the effort of the aged Abraham and Sarah, who hurried to set a banquet before strangers who happened to pass by during the heat of the day. It requires the serene detachment from the future of "our" hard-earned accomplishments even if they pass into the hands of fools, and the mastery of our self-righteous fugues when God blesses others more than we think they deserve.

Fear is perhaps the greatest obstacle to being a blessing. We mentioned some examples above—the fear that if we give to others, we will lack enough for ourselves; that giving will involve us with people with whom we are uncomfortable or will take us to places we assiduously avoid; or that we might appear naive and easily manipulated.

One story in the Bible reveals that the most surprising fear of all is the fear to reach out and *take* the biggest divine blessings. In Numbers 13–14, and its doublet in Deuteronomy 1:19–45, the Israelites at last reach the borders of the promised land after wandering in the wilderness for decades. God commands them to go up and take the promised land. Ten of the twelve spies sent to reconnoiter the new place note that it is a good land, but they emphasize potential dangers; they report that the inhabitants are giants, that they themselves seemed like grasshoppers to them, and that the people there live in huge, well-fortified cities, and so on. After this report, the people are too afraid to "go." Only two spies, Caleb and Joshua, say that they should take the land that God wants to give them.

Because of the difficulties and dangers that the project would involve and their fear of failure and even death, the people refuse to move toward the unimaginable gift—that land with cities, cisterns, and households that God prepared for them. Angered by their lack of faith, God condemns them to die in the wilderness. Only Caleb and Joshua are allowed to enter the land because they dared to trust that God was powerful enough to give a gift that was beyond human attainment.

For Christians, the promised land is an analogy for life with God, one that begins now and ends with everlasting union with the Grand Giver. Wonderful as this good news is, few *live* as if they really *believe* it. And rich as our existence may seem at the present, until we become a blessing for others we remain dull reflections of the splendid beings that God designed us to be. Unless we become icons of God, we waste the gift of a human life. We might as well be slugs whose possibilities are limited to the purview of their beady eyes as they creep along glued to the earth, leaving behind as their legacy a trace of muck.

Anthony de Mello's haunting story of "The Golden Eagle"[1] also urges us to go and be a blessing. It goes like this.

> A man found an eagle's egg and put it in
> the nest of a backyard hen. The eaglet

hatched with the brood of chicks and grew up with them.

All his life the eagle did what the backyard chickens did, thinking he was a backyard chicken. He scratched the earth for worms and insects. He clucked and cackled. And he would thrash his wings and fly a few feet into the air.

Years passed and the eagle grew very old. One day he saw a magnificent bird far above him in the cloudless sky. It glided in graceful majesty in the powerful wind currents, with scarcely a beat of its strong golden wings.

The old eagle looked up in awe. "Who's that?" he asked.

"That's the eagle, the king of the birds," said his neighbor. "He belongs to the sky. We belong to the earth—we're chickens."

So the eagle lived and died a chicken, for that's what he thought he was.

Notes

CHAPTER 1

    1. Although the names of Abram and Sarai are not changed to Abraham and Sarah until Genesis 17, throughout this work both are referred to by the more familiar names.

    2. The standard translation appears in the Septuagint, a second century BC Greek translation of the Hebrew Scriptures.

    3. The Greek for disciple, *mathaetaes*, means "learner."

CHAPTER 2

    1. Another familiar example of this type scene is found in Luke 1:39–45 where Mary, who is pregnant with Jesus, goes to visit her old cousin Elizabeth, who is preg-

nant with John the Baptist. When the women meet, the child in Elizabeth's womb recognizes Jesus and leaps for joy. Later John will recognize Jesus at the Jordan River and then go before him to announce his coming.

2. For a general overview of this concept, see, for example, Robert R. Wilson, "Genealogy, Genealogies," *The Anchor Bible Dictionary* (New York: Doubleday, 1992), Vol. 2, 929–32.

3. For more information on this connection, see U. Hübner, "Esau," *The Anchor Bible Dictionary*, Vol. 2, 574–75. See also Esau and Edom in Gen 36:1; Jer 49:8, 10; Mal 1:2–3; 1 Chr 1:35; Esau and Seir in Gen 27:11, 23; 32:4; 33:14–16; 36:6, 8; Deut 2:2–8, 12, 29; Josh 24:4.

4. The scholarly consensus is that the book of Genesis, like those of the rest of the Pentateuch, reached its present form around 400 BC, practically two hundred years after the fall of Judah to Babylon. Thus, by the time the narratives about Esau and Jacob are composed, their mutual animosity could have festered for at least this long.

5. See Gen 32:6–22, and Gen 33:1–14.

6. The vagueness of this conclusion results from the fact that the interpretation of this text is much discussed and debated. See comments on this pericope in such commentaries as, for example, that of Claus Westermann, *Genesis 12—36*, trans. John J. Scullion (Minneapolis: Augsburg Publishing House, 1985), 512–521.

7. In spite of several biblical claims that one cannot see God and live, most biblical personages do. See, for example, Judg 6:11–24; 13:15–23, etc.

8. Entertaining and obsequious examples of this can be found in the Amarna tablets, which are translated in, for example, J. B. Pritchard, *Ancient Near Eastern Texts Relating to the Old Testament* (Princeton University Press, 1969).

9. See "Forgiveness" in biblical dictionaries.

10. Esau's actions are very similar to those of another great forgiver, those of the prodigal son's father in Luke 15 who welcomes back the son who has squandered his share of the family possessions.

CHAPTER 3

1. Dag Hammarskjöld, *Markings*, trans. Leif Sjöberg and W. H. Auden (New York: Knopf, 1968), 197.

2. The Greek word for "pity" or "mercy" in Matthew 18:33 appears in the penitential rite of Christian liturgy in the phrase *"Kyrie, eleison"*; that is, "Lord, have mercy."

CHAPTER 4

1. For further reading on the topic of hospitality, see J. Koenig, *New Testament Hospitality* (Philadelphia: Fortress, 1985); and Gustav Stählin, "Xenos," in *Theological Dictionary of the New Testament* (Grand Rapids: Eerdmans, 1967), V:1–36.

2. For other type scenes of biblical hospitality see Gen 19:1–26; Judg 19; and Luke 7:36–50.

3. For example, in Gen 18:16–33, Abraham accompanies the Lord after the divine visit; it is then that they discuss the fate of Sodom and Gomorrah.

4. See, for example, Gen 14:14–15; 31:23; Exod 14:4, 8, 9, 23; Lev 26:17, 36, 37; Deut 1:44; 19:6; Josh 2:5, 7, 16, 22; 10:10; etc.; 1 Sam 17:52; 23:25, 28; 24:15; 26:18, 20; etc.

5. For a biblical example of a less perfect offer of hospitality, see Judg 19:15–18 in which the old man who finally invites the Levite and his unfortunate concubine to his house must first ask these questions of them.

6. For another example of this, see the respectful exchange between Abraham and the Hittites in Gen 23, where Abraham makes a deal to buy a burial cave for Sarah.

CHAPTER 5

1. Marian Wright Edelman, *Lanterns: A Memoir of Mentors* (Boston: Beacon Press, 1999), Lesson 21, 166–67.

CHAPTER 6

1. See Jan Lambrecht, *Out of the Treasure. The Parables in the Gospel of Matthew* (Grand Rapids: Eerdmans, 1991), 76.

2. John Donahue, *The Gospel in Parable* (Philadelphia: Fortress, 1988), 83–85.

3. Lambrecht, *Treasure*, 80.

4. John R. Donahue, *Gospel*, 83.

5. See John R. Donahue, "Tax Collector," in *The Anchor Bible Dictionary* (New York: Doubleday, 1992), 6:337–38, and other Bible dictionaries.

6. See Donahue, *Gospel*, 81–82.

7. "What belongs to you" is, in Greek, *to son*. Likewise in the parable of the talents in Matthew 25:25, *to son* is what the one-talent person gives back to the master: "I was afraid, and I went out and hid your talent in the ground. Here, you have what is yours *[to son]*." The master responds in 25:27: "Then you ought to have invested my money with the bankers, and on my return I would have received what was my own *[to 'emon]* with interest." Similarly, in Luke 15:31, the father reminds the older brother, "you are always with me, and all that is mine is yours" *[ta 'ema sa 'estin]*.

8. Lambrecht, *Treasure*, 82, which refers readers to Matthew 19:23–24, 29.

9. Lambrecht, *Treasure*, 76. See also 77–79.

10. Lambrecht, *Treasure*, 83.

11. Donahue, *Gospel*, 85.

12. Lambrecht, *Treasure*, 83–86.

EPILOGUE

1. William Dych, *Anthony de Mello* (Maryknoll, NY: Orbis Books 1999), 53–54.

ILLUMINATIONBOOKS

Other Books in the Series

Everyday Virtues
        by John W. Crossin, OSFS

The Mysteries of Light
        by Roland J. Faley, TOR

Healing Mysteries
        by Adrian Gibbons Koester

Carrying the Cross with Christ
        by Joseph T. Sullivan

Saintly Deacons
        by Deacon Owen F. Cumming

Finding God Today
        by E. Springs Steele

Hail Mary and Rhythmic Breathing
        by Richard Galentino

The Eucharist
        by Joseph M. Champlin

Gently Grieving
        by Constance M. Mucha

Devotions for Caregivers
        by Marilyn Driscoll